Transform

GO BEYOND CHANGE
Bless the Works of My Hands

21 DAY

Devotional & Journal

Transform
GO BEYOND CHANGE
Bless the Works of My Hands

21 DAY
Devotional & Journal

Published by Krystal Lee Enterprises (KLE Publishing)
Copyright © 2024 by K. Lee. All rights reserved.
Please send comments and questions:
Krystal Lee Enterprises
770-240-0089 Ext. 1
sales@KLEPub.com
To Reach the Author:
Email: me@drkrystallee.com me@authorklee.com
Web: AuthorKLee.com
Social Media All Channels: @AuthorKLee

Printed in the United States of America.
All rights reserved. No part of this book may be reproduced or transmitted in any form or by any means, electronic or mechanical, including photocopying, recording, or any information storage and retrieval system without written permission of the publisher except for brief quotations used in reviews, written specifically for inclusion in a newspaper, blog, magazine, or academic paper.

ISBN: 978-1-945066-56-6

Transform Go Beyond Change

So this book was written as an answer to those who find themselves READY to transform their lives and go beyond change! If you have been saying you want your life to change, and you have being doing things, but your life hasn't transformed, I invite you to this table! We can make a lot of changes but they all don't lead to transformation do they?

We can switch out a man and have the same relationship. We can get a new business and do well, but we still feel empty. We can eat a feast, cook a meal, go to parties, have sex, and still it not give us the life we are looking for. If you want to breathe and feel alive, transforming your life is the only way. You need a new wind, a renewed perspective about your purpose and reason for being. You need to reconnect with the source.

A chicken can run for a while with its head cut off, but in the end, it dies. The chicken is unaware of its morbid state, and although it is moving, it is already dead. Quicken your spirit today. Do you know we have a God on our side that can speak to the dead?

He can make dead bones live again. He can transform your life and make it better than it ever was. He can restore you, deliver you from your past, and renew you from the inside out. This is not a outward makeover, this is a inner transformation. This is surgery of the heart, mind, body, and will! This is a soul transformation!

If you need to live on purpose and start with self-healing and spiritual growth and then move to projects like writing your book, starting your business, going back to school, and getting your confidence back to take dominion, this is the banner and motto to empower your life.

You have everything you need to transform your life! You were born with a purpose, on purpose, for a purpose. Keep Transforming, and Go Beyond Change!

Welcome to the Transform and Go Beyond Change devotional series with Dr. Krystal Lee (Dr. K)! I am excited to have you here and welcome you to connect and journey with me as I help you implement the goals and purpose of your life. Let's connect and grow together.

Here's a sample of what is to come! Scan the QR to use free and paid resources to journey through this devotional and journal experience.

Transform

GO BEYOND CHANGE
Bless the Works of My Hands

21 DAY

Devotional & Journal

Table of Contents

INTRODUCTION	7
DAY 1	17
DAY 2	25
DAY 3	33
DAY 4	41
DAY 5	49
DAY 6	57
DAY 7	65
DAY 8	73
DAY 9	81
DAY 10	89
DAY 11	97
DAY 12	105
DAY 13	113
DAY 14	121
DAY 15	129
DAY 16	137
DAY 17	145
DAY 18	153
DAY 19	161
DAY 20	169
DAY 21	177

3 And he told them many things in parables, saying: "A sower went out to sow. **4** And as he sowed, some seeds fell along the path, and the birds came and devoured them. **5** Other seeds fell on rocky ground, where they did not have much soil, and immediately they sprang up, since they had no depth of soil, **6** but when the sun rose they were scorched. And since they had no root, they withered away. **7** Other seeds fell among thorns, and the thorns grew up and choked them. **8** Other seeds fell on good soil and produced grain, some a hundredfold, some sixty, some thirty. **9** He who has ears, let him hear."

Introduction Matt 13:3-9

The Father is faithful in placing His Word on man's heart, but are we faithful in listening? Do we allow the cares of this life to choke out the word? Do we allow people to distract us? Do we allow bills, lawsuits, fear, the rumbling in our stomachs, or another loud distraction to steal away His position in our lives? Does sleep rob you of having 10 minutes with God each morning? Does TV steal your nights or social media scrolling?

I can tell you, if we are all honest, we each make time for what we want to do. What has a hold on us has no problem with demanding our time, either. Our submission to pursue these needs, desires, wants, and cravings is unapologetic. What are we missing from our lives–that should have us on our knees–especially if we are in the valley of lack is time with the King. Yah, God Almighty is above every king on earth. He is the Creator, and everything is beneath His feet. However, is that true for you, for us?

I can say there have been many times that if it had not been for me being a priority of Yah, I would have found myself still repeating a scarcity mindset. I remember what Yah (God) has done for me to make it through a rough patch. At the same time that I was evicted from my apartment, not even two weeks later, I lost my car because it was repossessed–but God gave them both back! I cleared up the payment I owed to the previous apartment, and I was able to clear my debt completely and get my vehicle back after a repossession. The truth is you can start life over, even when you feel like life has hit a brick wall.

I must confess that when I experienced heavy burdens that plagued my financial existence, it was linked to an area that was out of order in my life. It doesn't have to

Introduction

be a sin always—but oftentimes, it is. I remember during the time I was evicted and lost my car, I was trying to make a relationship work with my youngest daughter's dad.

Anytime he and I made up and thought to give things another shot, my life would implode. I couldn't blame the devil—I started to see that it was God! When He is not happy with our choices, He is not shy about correcting you and getting your attention by any means. I got tired of losing things and getting setback after setback, so I decided to put the Word back at the foundation of my life. I no longer leaned on my ideas for what I needed to fix as a problem.

Too often, we think we need a person, a job, money, or something outside of our control to align our lives with our perceived direction. It was when I made the Word more than just a bible I carried around, more than something that I kept in my heart and half followed. I had to commit to surrendering my life to follow as best as I could. How many of us know I wasn't given my best?

I could have—and it was a must to apply the principles I knew to shift the direction of my life. There are many reasons why our lives are not blessed or the works of our hands. For some of us, there is sin in the camp. If you are living a life of sin and you don't plan on changing, mercy can be on your life, but you won't have the blessing. You want God the Father to be well pleased with you, don't you? You want to receive the blessing, then!

Question

Do you feel like there is more that you can give God? What areas in your life could you invite Him in to help you change? Write them down here.

Introduction

Esau was mad because he gave up the blessing for a bowl of beans. He was content with the things until the things lost their value. What are you giving up the blessing for? A car, a man, a job, a fantasy, or something else? At the end of the day, nothing is worth replacing a walk with God!

He can change everything and keep you speechless about His goodness. If He told you that every day you read, pursue, and study this book, I will give you $100. How many of us would be committed to doing it daily? How many of you know He has more than that in store for you?

Like the parable in the bible, the owner said if you work in my field, I will give you this amount for the day. He did that for everyone who came at any time. How many of us know the Presence of God is more than the pay we get for the day? I am sure He did things like bring them water and food, show them kindness, and so much more.

He is the God of overflow and abundance!

Prayer

> "Father, thank you for meeting us where we are. Some of us will be 100% committed, and others will struggle. May You show us mercy as we learn to value Your Word. As we strive to make time for You, help us see how we can incorporate You more into our lives. Help us not to feel guilty as we work to balance our dedication to You and the things we are struggling to let go of. Give us enough peace and balance to carve out the time You need for each entry. Help us to have the right heart as we read and study to hear, believe, and implement the wisdom given in this book and throughout this journey! In your precious son's name, Yashua (aka Jesus), we say hallelujah, and So be it!"

Affirmation — "I have a Word that is working in my life that reminds me I am valuable no matter what I am facing today."

Reflection

> *Was there anything you wanted to remember from this reading? Take a second and write it down. Your writing helps to connect your feelings and understanding. Ponder on the reading, questions, and reflections each day.*

Notes

Introduction

I end my prayers with hallelujah because it means we seek the Father's direction on what to do next. I say, "So be it," sometimes because what we have prayed is established and heard, and God will determine what shall be. I do not say "amen" because it has historical connections to pagan deities that I don't care to acknowledge them.

However, with the prayers, use the words you are comfortable with. I also use the Hebrew names to address God and Jesus (Yashua) because they are personal to me, and the scriptures say there is power in His Name, so I honor that. However, do what the Father leads you to do as you pray. I do use Yah and God interchangeably so everyone can know who I am referencing.

Before we embark on this journey, I must ask: Do you know Yah to be the God of overflow? Do you want to know Him like that? Okay, for those serious, do you NEED to know Him like that? Great! Enjoy this 21-day journey with me as I help you to reflect and implement principles, verses, and thought points to transform your life with Yah.

Choosing to take God at His Word was the best decision I have ever made. I know that He is the one who has pulled me single-handedly out of poverty, want, lack of confidence, inferiority, eliminated my anxiety about the future, and lays me down–and wakes me up with peace. If you want and need that in your life, travel with me and engage yourself in this book.

The way this devotional is outlined, you will read a passage, the talk points, and a prayer daily. I encourage you to log your thoughts each day to keep up with your progress because you will not remember everything if you don't write it down. So use the notes section as you read (there are lines to write in this book!), answer the short questions, and at the end of the day (or throughout the day), jot down things that happened that answered prayer, wowed you or made you grateful.

After you complete this journey, I want you to do it again and have someone do it with you! Something happens when we pray in numbers. Also, to help you with this devotional, I have additional resources for this 21-day journey you can participate online. I will read the verse, go over the thought point, and help you go through the book!

I will not leave room for you to fail. If you get off schedule, don't worry; just catch up. Try to complete this book in 30 days. So if you miss a day, it's okay, but don't stop and commit to finishing it in 30 days. This book is meant to help you form habits, ingrain a committed time for God, and improve yourself and those around you. You need this, and my heart desires to help you through it.

I know you are ready to start Day 1 to Transform and Go Beyond Change now, but you can begin tomorrow since you have been doing so well so far! As we embark on this journey, review the reflection and write notes after the daily reading and what you experience on each day. Write the date on the pink line at the top of each chapter to track your progress. I will see you tomorrow as we begin Day 1.

15 Make us glad for as many days as you have afflicted us, and for as many years as we have seen evil. **16** Let your work be shown to your servants, and your glorious power to their children. **17** Let the favor of the Lord our God be upon us, and establish the work of our hands upon us; yes, establish the work of our hands!

Day 1 Psalm 90:15-17

Day 1

Can I get a witness that we have all seen evil in our day? People who have stolen from us, lied to us, or tried to inflict harm on us–on purpose. If you have worked any job, it seems that it takes hours for someone to latch on to you and determine to make your life hell. They seem to have no reason to dislike us, but the deep-seated dislike is there.

They point out our flaws. Our shortcomings are not gently corrected but plastered as a strong reprimand. We can grow frustrated with people like this and loathe our jobs, and for some, even question our existence. We may think that this person is right or that I deserve the treatment I am getting because I did mess up.

Psalms 91 is a chapter dedicated to the protection of those who read it. We pray Psalms 91 over our lives because we all have something that is trying to steal, kill, or devour us or something we love. No matter if it is internal (in our thoughts, hearts, or emotions) or external (dealing with people, jobs, experiences, or circumstances), we need Yah (God) to show up in our lives.

We need Him to gently remind us that we belong to Him–even in our imperfections. Yes, we can make mistakes and miss the mark completely, but God can and does smile upon us. He wants to still help us to grow and shower His favor, which we need, on our lives. With the favor of God, you don't have to be perfect!

Day 1

You don't have to get it all right to still make and be blessed by your work. I remember when I sewed my first and last costume for a client. I was scared about the results because I knew it had flaws. I knew I struggled with the piece, but the favor was on it. The client loved it! She said, "This is the best-made costume I ever purchased!" I was shocked. I can never forget that princess ballgown I made as a project that met a need I had financially and a faith experience I trusted Yah through.

Sometimes, we have to jump out there and put out what we have and not worry about perfection. We give life our best and learn what we can as we advance. The books I publish today are much better than the books I did before. What has not changed is my heart. I can see the same power in my old books, and the graphics and new tricks I have learned have improved my books–yes, but the same favor I still have from Yah to write is in them all.

Question

Do you feel there is someone pointing a finger at you? It can be on the job, in business, politics, family, or otherwise. What is the accusation or the lie? What do you feel you need to bring about resolution?

Prayer

> *"Father, I thank You all the more because You are mindful and care about us. Adonia (Lord), we bring before You the issues we have with co-workers, clients, family members, or others who are hyper-critical of us. Those who find fault in us and make us second guess Your favor on our lives. We thank You, Father, that in situations where our best may not be enough, You will provide a way for us to learn and still grow. Thank You for turning trials in our lives into stepping stones for our success. Help fine-tune our vision and our heart to see you and learn Your truth. Empower us to live out the purpose You put in our lives each day at a time. In the name of Yashua, we say thank you, hallelujah, and so be it."*

Affirmation   "Yah knows how to make every trial, lesson, or situation bless His plans for my life, so I won't quit moving forward no matter the challenges before me."

Reflection

> *Are there areas in your life where you feel you are too hard on yourself? Have others been hyper-critical of your work to the point where you question your abilities? Don't let them discourage you from trying, and be open to learning better ways to advance your objectives. The favor of God is on your life! Write down your thoughts from this entry in the notes!*

Notes

10 And all the peoples of the earth shall see that you are called by the name of the Lord, and they shall be afraid of you. **11** And the Lord will make you abound in prosperity, in the fruit of your womb and in the fruit of your livestock and in the fruit of your ground, within the land that the Lord swore to your fathers to give you. **12** The Lord will open to you his good treasury, the heavens, to give the rain to your land in its season and to bless all the work of your hands. And you shall lend to many nations, but you shall not borrow. **13** And the Lord will make you the head and not the tail, and you shall only go up and not down, if you obey the commandments of the Lord your God, which I command you today, being careful to do them,

Day 2 Deut. 28:10-13

Day 2

I love this passage because many of us have heard pieces of this passage that have given us hope over the years. You will be the lender, not the borrower. You will be the head and not the tail. What I find to be a vital part of this passage is you will only see these blessings if you observe the commandments of God!

How many of us skip that verse or have never heard it? This is a huge disservice to believers because we don't understand why nations need us and why we must strive to live right. We know that living right will bless us, but we don't understand the importance of how living right will impact others. Do you know when you live right, you put fear in other people--the kingdom of darkness?

I know you have seen movies where the bad guys are afraid to touch nuns and people who look like God. I am not arguing religious practices here, but people who have the Spirit of God on their lives people take notice. Even in the bible, the wise guy says if these people really do serve God, there is nothing you can do to stop them. It is better that God judge them than for us to get involved unless we will be fighting against God (Acts 5:38-39).

If you keep working to look more like Christ, He will do the work to make you look more like Him. The work that Yah starts in you, He is willing and able to finish it (Philippians 1:6)! So be bold about serving God and wanting to get things in order. As you start changing your life and removing people or things you used to do, take courage! Yah, got you, even if no one else does.

When we start committing to upgrade our mindset to look like and be like Christ, He will make you abound! I know a woman who quit her job. Things weren't working out, and she wasn't happy anymore. She thought she would get a job soon after, but guess what happened? She started to feel inferior by the job process. She thought that her skill set wasn't enough.

She desired to go back to school, but she didn't have the money. Do you know that God gave her the money from her daughter to return to school, and she passed her insurance exam on the first try? Look at God! But she still doesn't have a job. She didn't want to go door to door, and she didn't want to work hourly. She wanted to be her own boss.

After getting several offers from companies who said she had to buy her own leads, she stopped looking and laid on the couch more. She started to lose her confidence. But she kept hearing me say, "What do you want?" She got back to reading and speaking the Word as she was near losing her house. She committed to this process, and she got a job in days after committing–not just with anyone, but she gets paid weekly, works her own hours, and she works for a company that provides her with free leads they pay for!

With her house, she had a year of deferment, and when she couldn't pay a year later, they put her in another process that delayed her payments for two more months. By then, her new offer kicked in, her money was flowing, and she is kicking butt now in her new career in life insurance. If you need a breakthrough–right now, don't be surprised if the first step to bless your hands is to bless your mind! You need to renew your mind and know that this is the same God that parted the Red Sea! He makes miracles happen when He is given the room to MOVE in your life!

So yes, the Father can bless you no matter where you are and how low you might feel. He can eliminate struggle and bring you the blessing. Keep journeying through implementing His commandments, and let's see your transformation take place.

Remember to scan the QR to use free and paid resources to journey through this devotional and journal experience.

Question

Do you trust God? Do you feel He can be Your source and connect You to whatever and whoever You need? Why or why not?

Prayer

> "Father, today we must thank You for being God! The One who is over everything, who has it all and is everything we need and more. We bring before You our needs today. Our desires because we know You care about them. Father, we need You to bless the works of our hands and help us in our jobs and in our businesses. To honor us before man and to encourage us as we strive to implement Your commandments in our lives. We know it takes faith to please You, and we have faith that You can change our situation. Thank You for increasing our faith if what we have is not enough. We know that You are more than enough, and the prayers of the righteous avail much! In the name of Your son, Yashua, we say thank You, and it is done."

Affirmation — "God has everything I need to change my situation, and I will not allow anything to change my belief that He is for me."

Reflection

> *What do you need the Father to touch? Is it your money? A job? Resources? Your heart? He can do it! Write down your needs with passion, and remember to pray through it!*

Notes

1 O God, you are my God; earnestly I seek you; my soul thirsts for you; my flesh faints for you, as in a dry and weary land where there is no water. **2** So I have looked upon you in the sanctuary, beholding your power and glory. **3** Because your steadfast love is better than life, my lips will praise you. **4** So I will bless you as long as I live; in your name, I will lift up my hands.

Day 3 Psalm 63:1-4

Day 3

It is easy for people to complain and remind whoever listens how things are wrong in our lives. We see the issues so quickly, but if we point them out and forget to dance about things going well, we miss a big opportunity. You tell us to enter into Your gates with thanksgiving and Your courts with praise (Psalms 100:4). I am overjoyed to see You working in other people's lives.

If we are honest, we can be happy for others, but we still struggle to be happy if we don't see the blessing in our own lives. If you are struggling to see the glory and power of Yah, don't shrink back. Don't run from the feeling, the thought, but realize there is more in God that you have yet to see. He is deep and can go deeper than we all can imagine. If you feel that you have a shallow connection that isn't producing, you have to ask, "Why?"

When we are babies in Christ, things will come easier than when He wants to advance our journey. We may think we can be a baby forever. You can't. He will not allow you to grow stagnant. Your worship will stink like stagnant water. He wants the fruit of your lips, even when you are going through, even through the challenges we are facing. He wants to test you to see if the lessons are being learned.

Can you praise Him when things are going bad? Can you drink from His well if that means going through comes with it? Will you keep seeking Him when things are not going well, your bank account dwindles, and your heart

Day 3

fails? We read that His love is steadfast. The love of Yah is never-ending and all-powerful.

Stay encouraged. The Father is here with you. When you cry, He is here to catch your tears and walk with you through these moments with you. He wants you to learn from Him and know the fruit of your lips will carry you when you feel empty. When you lift praise, you are buying food and drinks with no money (Isiah 55:1)!

Are you waiting for things to be perfect to give Yah Praise? If you are waiting for the right atmosphere, for the music to play, and for you to have the unction, you are missing a powerful tool to change your surroundings. You confuse the devil when you can praise Him while you suffer. Job said, "Why you slay me, I will still trust in You" (Job 12:15).

It may please the Father for you to go through the fire. For you to learn humility and unconditional love. It is one thing to say you love someone, but another to learn how to love someone. We show that we love Him not just with what we do when we are happy but also when we are challenged. True parenting requires the instruction of both. You can give them everything they want and ignore what they need. We need to be able to weather the storm just as much as we enjoy the sun.

If you believe the Father is slow to deliver, know that He can change life in a moment. Our heart, gratitude, or the lack thereof, can delay our timing in a situation. Sometimes, we have to go through the storm because it won't blow away. When you sing, clap your hands, dance, and worship through the process, you will get strength.

Can you imagine the true power behind Kumbayah? When you see people being sold, burned, whipped, spat upon, or jumping to drown in the ocean–how much you wanted Yah to Come by Here!

Singing songs helps us to reconnect with the power, the history, and the Hand of Yah that still extends toward people. Some things we have to live through so the people on the other side can marvel at the great work Yah was doing throughout. Life may not always be easy, but the Father knows how to send us a break even through the worst of times.

Question

Do you feel the love of God in your life? Do you sing a song of gratitude and worship through the ups and downs? Will you make room for Him even when He feels distant from you?

Prayer

> "Yah, we thank You today for putting a joyful noise in our mouths. You are good and so worthy of Praise. Some of the songs we grew up singing or that find their way into our hearts, thank You for allowing them to raise our hearts and bring peace. Continue to speak to us in song and give us the heart and mind to worship with the fruits of our lips. Yah, You mean more to us than we can ever imagine. Thank You for giving us what we need to carry on and make it through the test. For healing our families, careers, jobs, businesses, and finances on today. Thank You for blessing the works of our hands. Shalom."

Affirmation   "Even though my day might be hard, with a joyful heart, You make it easier and show me how to smile through any pain...I will be light as a feather."

Reflection

> *Name your favorite song to worship Yah (God), and I want you to hum it. When it feels good to your soul, sing it aloud. Make a library of songs you like. Here are a few to get you started!*
>
> - *I hear the Sound - Maurette Brown Clark*
> - *God is - Melvin Cripell*
> - *Press in Your Presence - Shana Wilson*

Notes

8 But now, O Lord, you are our Father; we are the clay, and you are our potter; we are all the work of your hand. **9** Be not so terribly angry, O Lord, and remember not iniquity forever. Behold, please look. We are all your people. **10** Your holy cities have become a wilderness; Zion has become a wilderness, Jerusalem a desolation. **11** Our holy and beautiful house, where our fathers praised you, has been burned by fire, and all our pleasant places have become ruins. **12** Will you restrain yourself at these things, O Lord? Will you keep silent and afflict us so terribly?

Day 4 Isaiah 64:8-12

Day 4

When life is a challenge, the number one thing we ask that the Father do is intervene. For some of us, our families are a mess. Children disrespect their parents, the parents hate their parents, and the chaos continues from generation to generation. It is the enemy's plan to sift us as wheat (Luke 22:31), to tear down families and have us function backward, for up to be down, and right to be wrong, and life to be a mess.

But we serve a God that does things in decency and in order (1 Corinthians 14:4). When the house tears down, there is something that was out of order. When things are out of order, they can be seen by everyone, but when does the Father get involved? When we line up with His desire.

Do you know crying and calling on God is good, but if you have not aligned your heart to His plan, He doesn't hear the prayers of sinners (John 9:31)? Yah wants to hear the worshipper and from the people who are doing His will. He says, "If My people, which are called by My name, shall humble themselves, and pray, and seek My Face, and turn from their wicked ways; then will I hear from heaven, and will forgive their sin, and will heal their land" (2 Chronicles 7:14).

Many of us have lived in shambles because we refuse to give Yah access to enter into our lives and work out our situations. We want the help of God but not the direction. We want the goodness but not the correction. We have to understand that if our lives are in desolation and we are

Day 4

in the wilderness, not knowing which way is right, we need a foundation.

We need Yah to enter into our situation and bring order. Boundaries are not the devil, and hearing "no" when we need it is not oppression. Some of us are asking, "How long, Father, will you wait, and how much has to go wrong before you get involved?" We have been made in His likeness, and we are afforded rights and privileges that give us the right to choose our life's direction. The Bible records how the Father suggests, we choose life (Deuteronomy 30:9)!

The choices we make can be making room for the hell prevailing in our lives. We can speak to the storm, as our Advocate has already demonstrated. But will you dare to open your mouth to speak to the storm?

Faith is the things hoped for but are not yet seen (Hebrews 11:1-3). When life looks its worst, this is the best time to praise Him. If you want His attention, I dare you to worship Him in spirit and in truth! Then, when He speaks to your spirit, do what He tells you to do. The more you worship, listen, and do, the stronger your confidence becomes to where you can worship through any storm.

Question

> What is happening around you that you need Yah to take authority over? Are you speaking the Word daily and thanking God for doing it? Are you waiting to see it or operating by faith?

Prayer

> *"Wow, Father. You have made today a great day. Although the storm is raging around me in this area of my life, I will still trust You, like Job. I will give You my heart's attention and allow You to set the bar for my expectations. I will give You the fruit of my lips even in this difficult situation because I know You can change and walk me through it. You are bigger than my problems, and Your Heart towards me is to see me look more like You! I trust Your guidance, and I place Your ways above my own. I will forsake all other opinions and focus on Yours. In the name of your son, Yashua Jesus the Christ, hallelujah, and so be it."*

Affirmation *"There is no problem around me You cannot solve, so I put my full confidence in You."*

Reflection

> *What are some of your thoughts after reading this entry? What scriptures are there you can use to help correct your situation? What areas would you like to include in our prayer today? Jot them down, and let's pray.*

Notes

19 Oh, how abundant is your goodness, which you have stored up for those who fear you and worked for those who take refuge in you, in the sight of the children of mankind! **20** In the cover of your presence, you hide them from the plots of men; you store them in your shelter from the strife of tongues. **21** Blessed be the Lord, for he has wondrously shown his steadfast love to me when I was in a besieged city.

Day 5 Psalm 31:19-21

Day 5

Those who fear the Lord are wise. He is grand, all-powerful, and all-knowing. Nothing happens on earth or in the earth that He does not know. Knowing how big He is helps you keep yourself in perspective, people, and your problems or circumstances. Nothing is too hard for God.

Taking refuge in the promises and power of Yah is the best choice. The Father knows how to pull out things on the inside of you. He has put them there for when you need them most.

As we study and honor Him with our lives, He will reveal to us more of Himself but even more about who we are in Him. We learn to appreciate His goodness with the more we learn about ourselves, too. We are not perfect, but His perfect love helps us to see the best in ourselves, our situations, and even others.

When we see the world through His eyes, we can glean how important it is to have Him as a covering. The wings of the Almighty are so vast that they can cover cities, states, and property. I remember living in Florida and going through a number of storms, hurricanes, and tornadoes.

It was a prayer always to keep the windows from bursting out and losing water or electricity. I remember this one year, trees were going down left and right. From our window, we saw the lightning strike the tree and heard the biggest thud as the tree slaps down on cars underneath. We had the lights out and portable lights on.

Day 5

It was like camping indoors, and partly, it was fun to slow down life and be inside with family and friends. We talked all night as we heard the winds blowing, the rain falling, and objects tussling around in the storm. Every once in a while, a stick would hit the door, or a bang would happen that would have Carlos (my best friend's brother) run out of his room and say, "Did y'all hear that?"

Even when the city was under attack by the weather, my faith and trust were in Yah (God). I remember praying over everyone before it happened. After the storm had passed, when we all came outside to look at the damage, it was a miracle that my car was completely spared. Nothing was on it but leaves!

My best friend Nancy's car had a branch land right across it, and we were sure it was totaled. The best part was that she could use her insurance and get the car she needed because the one she had was stalling, and the trade-in value wasn't much based on the condition. But good old insurance and gap insurance came through, and she got what she needed to zoom around Orlando a bit longer.

One thing I love about Yah is that no matter what you are going through, He will make everything work for the good of those who love Him and are called according to His purpose. Nancy and I needed different things, and we found a way to make our experiences unique, although we experienced the same storm. You in a marriage can go through the same issue and respond differently. You can be on a job and make the same mistake and get a different outcome.

Life isn't always fair, is it? But that is okay. No matter what end of the stick you get in life's draw, the Father will help you win. Think about that a bit more as you write your notes from this entry, and let's pray!

How are things going so far? Can I ask you to share your feedback and journey so far? Please scan the QR or use the url below to share your feedback or leave a review.

AuthorKLee.com/bless-works-of-my-hands-21-day

Question

> *What is happening around you that you need Yah to take authority over? Are you speaking the Word daily and thanking God for doing it? Are you waiting to see it or operating by faith?*

Prayer

> *"With gratitude, we come to You today. We lay our burdens down, and we bring our problems and situations before You with a heart of gratitude and fully confident that You want to help us, Lord. We know that no matter the war, problem, or situation, a Word from You can change everything. We are asking You to get involved in our lives. Help us to see what we are missing. Thank You for all the times You have saved us that we were unaware of. Thank You for the mercy and grace that You have shown in my life. Keep my heart on the right things so that I do not miss You and can capture my praise report to share with others. In the precious name of Yahsua, we pray. Hallelujah!"*

Affirmation — *"No matter my test, I thank you for rescuing me, keeping me through the storm, and blessing me to continue on."*

Reflection

> *What would you like to record on today? How are you feeling? What would you like to bring to the King of Kings? Jot it down and let me know how I can pray with you beyond today.*
>
> *#drk21day*

Notes

11 Behold, all who are incensed against you shall be put to shame and confounded; those who strive against you shall be as nothing and shall perish. **12** You shall seek those who contend with you, but you shall not find them; those who war against you shall be as nothing at all. **13** For I, the Lord your God, hold your right hand; it is I who say to you, "Fear not, I am the one who helps you."

Day 6 Isaiah 41:11-13

Day 6

The last man standing is the winner of any game or show we enjoy watching. We are glued to the tv set or phone to see who will pull off the win we feel is the win of the century. Yet we are unaware of the largest battle that has been fought and won--the battle that was fought to liberate us from sin and death, that heals, saves, and delivers.

We are here looking at the storms that are raging and yelling in our direction, distracting us from seeing the battle–or, more importantly, the results. The biggest game that is still underway and being played on you and me is the game we tip-toe around because many of us are unaware that we have already won!

Have you ever seen a show where the unlikely candidate wins? If the music doesn't play to trigger the ending, if we don't hear the clapping, see the people standing up and jumping up and down, we would swear the show didn't end even though we heard the announcement. When Christ died on the cross, many didn't stand up. Many didn't bow a knee. Too many hung their head and walked away because He didn't make a spectacle.

He appeared to have died in an uneventful way. They wanted a show with strobe lights and catchy music to play to trigger the emotion we fiend for to denote the end and promote an important moment in life. Isn't it amazing that if a lie is presented on the right plate, we will believe the lie over our own senses and reality?

Day 6

I love watching episodes on tv when chefs make food using the same ingredients, but they put a twist on it. They use the main flavors, but they add in other ingredients to allow a savory dish to be sweet, a dinner to be dessert, and the list goes on and on. We like the spice to the dish; it satisfies our palate with the taste we are familiar with, but the dish is a reinvented dish, another thing, like another gospel.

We are settling for ideas and thoughts that are not true. As for the word fiend, do you know what the dictionary says about it? There are several definitions, but the top one is demon, devil, or evil spirit. The second is a person who is extremely wicked, cruel, or unprincipled. The third is a person who is enthusiastically devoted to something, such as an addict or a fresh-air fiend. Lastly, a mischievous or spiteful person, especially a child. Wow, when I read this, the message opened wide. This word was founded in 1150 and is inherited from Germanic, and this word is synonymous with demon, devil, monster, and ogre.

Can you believe that? We have songs that say I am a fiend for you, dope fiend, and all kinds of craziness that we think to assimilate in the Gospel and in the sharing of the Word of God. Let me tell you, if you look around, the only one that will remain is the Word of God! No other Word will exalt itself above the Word of God!

Now that we know the power of Yah is stronger than any monster, ogre, devil, witch, or warlock, what does the Word say about you? Just a stanza above this one it tells us that Yah will not throw us away. He is calling us back into fellowship with Him no matter where we have went off to. The Bible records in this chapter of Isaiah 41, "Don't be afraid, for I am with you; don't be discouraged, for I am your God. I will strengthen you and help you! I will hold you up with my victorious right hand!"

If you are struggling right now, I want to encourage you that Yah is here working it out for you already. If you've felt like you are being chased or like someone is running you down, know when you turn around, nothing will be there. Your mind is playing tricks on you, and the enemy, the devil, is behind it. The accuser of the brethren is bringing up your pass and trying to bring you back there because he can't get close to your future!

If you are in the light, you will shine! Step into the light and jot down what you will hand over to Yah today so that He can deliver you with His victorious right Hand!

Question

Do you realize how powerful the Word of Yah is? Do you know who the Word is? How do you understand salvation? What does it mean to you? Are you saved?

Prayer

> *"Father, we thank You today that we can come boldly to the throne of grace. We are running to Your strong tower to help fight our battles. We know that You are stronger than our problems. That Your Word delivers, saves, and restores lives. Even though the devil thought to accuse me, he can no longer stand in my presence because Yahshua (Jesus), the living Word, has already paid it all! I am set free and delivered from all my wrong, and accept the Word You have spoken over my life. I accept Your help and promise to deliver me with Your Right Hand! All I can say is thank You. So be it, in the name of Yashua, Jesus the Christ."*

Affirmation

"I trust that God will avenge any wrong done to me—and because of His power and might, I can focus on being obedient and not fighting battles that are not mine."

Reflection

> *What do you need the Father to do? Who are your enemies? What is the problem? Do you believe Yah is fighting the battle for you? Rest in peace, knowing that all is well.*

Notes

16 Be not afraid when a man becomes rich, when the glory of his house increases. **17** For when he dies he will carry nothing away; his glory will not go down after him. **18** For though, while he lives, he counts himself blessed—and though you get praise when you do well for yourself— **19** his soul will go to the generation of his fathers who will never again see light. **20** Man in his pomp yet without understanding is like the beasts that perish.

Day 7 Psalm 49:16-20

Day 7

Wow, wow! This passage had me rocked when I first read Psalms 49 for the inclusion in this book! I was speechless and the reflection on the things the Father said, had me too ready to write more. I had to pull it in to select this section, but I love what comfort it can bring to encourage you to keep working.

This book has a position to bless the works of your hands but to do that we need to keep our eyes on our own race. I know we can look to the left and the right and see others making it doing all kinds of things. Some have left the flock to chase after other gods, things, riches, and possessions. Yet, the Word has already sealed their ending.

People who stray away from Yah, God Almighty, will find themselves dying no different than an animal. Yes, it is possible to do lots of things while you are here on earth. You can build cities with your name on it. You can buy mansions, houses, cars, Rolex watches, and all that your heart desires. You can go to concerts, have the best seats, and do all that your heart is contended to do, but when you die!

You see, we all have to get to that point where we account for how we lived our lives. The women you had, the men you dated, and the money you acquired will not help plead your case. You will have works that will go through the fire and amount to nothing. You will not impress the King of Kings who rules and governs over all; you would have wasted your time. The enemy is not after

Day 7

your stuff but your time!

We all have a limited supply of it, and how we use it matters. The Bible tells us the parable of the wise virgins who kept oil for their lamps so they would be ready for the bride-groom when he came. The ones who were playing around and wasting their oil had none left when he came, so they thought to borrow from those who had. Only they said "No, you have to go back and get more"–but there was no time!

I don't want to beat you over the head or make you feel guilty; I want you to see that the time to work so the Father can bless you is now. It is not when you get more money, get a better job, or get something you have asked for; it is when you feel you don't have enough. It is for when you feel tired; it is for when you feel inadequate.

You will not be able to go and borrow the works of other people for God to bless you. I know that when we participate in group projects, sometimes, a few do most of the work while others do nothing but get a grade. In the Kingdom, we all have to work! If you want the wealth that the Father affords to His children, He wants His children to be multipliers. He is not looking for the lazy, the foolish, and the unfruitful steward. He wants those who are intentional about their time and resources.

When the disciples finished serving the people, they didn't leave the leftovers on the ground; they sent baskets and picked them up to have more for another day. The Father will keep on giving, but are you a dame who blocks all the wealth He has already given you so overflow is not necessary? Are you content with what you have, where you are with Him, and all that is around you?

If only the children of God knew all His plans for them, surely they would not choose to die like animals or look and envy those who obtain riches by doing evil. They would be too focused on doing His good work and obtaining favor from Him rather than man.

Question

> *How many things has the Father asked you to do, and you replied, "Let me go back and do that now?" How often do we say, "I will do that later," and later never comes? How often do you think you waste time on things that will not add up?*

Prayer

"Father, help me today to make better use of my time. I have been looking at others You've blessed, and I want Your blessing on my life. I no longer look at anyone with envy, nor will I spend a lot of time looking at what others may boast about, but I will boast in Your goodness. I will keep my heart from distractions and keep my focus set on pleasing You and not the world. I will work as unto the Lord because my reward is with You. I thank You today for cleaning my heart, renewing my focus, and keeping me mindful of how I spend my time and resources."

Affirmation — *"You are the provider of every breath that I take, and I thank You for giving me life so that I may serve You all the more."*

Reflection

> *What can you do today with your time that God can bless? Can you spend time with your children, husband, co-workers, or others doing something the Father would be pleased with? Like what?*

Notes

5 Thus says God, the Lord, who created the heavens and stretched them out, who spread out the earth and what comes from it, who gives breath to the people on it and spirit to those who walk in it: **6** "I am the Lord; I have called you in righteousness; I will take you by the hand and keep you; I will give you as a covenant for the people, a light for the nations, **7** to open the eyes that are blind, to bring out the prisoners from the dungeon, from the prison those who sit in darkness.

Day 8 Isaiah 42:5-7

Day 8

This is great news for everyone who wants to impact the world. Did you see what I saw in this passage? The Father wants to use you and your individual gift to lift up nations! To encourage the many who are blind to open their eyes so they can see. For setting those held prisoner to their own thoughts, judgments, feelings, and disappointments, free! He wants to use you to be an ordinary superhero because His power will work on the inside of you.

I know sometimes we can think, "Will what I have impact the world and the Kingdom at the same time?" We may think of asking Father to bless our hands so that we can use money to solve problems–but not everything needs money. Some of us need people to enter our lives and coach us, others to encourage us with a word, and more of us to hear love in someone's words and actions.

When you are used to feeling low, it can mean the world to get a simple gesture of hope to signal that you matter on this earth here and now. You are not a mistake, and your hard work is not being overlooked. If you are the one chosen to give a smile to someone getting their nails down and hear them talk, listen. If you are the stylist, using your hands to do hair, take the time to listen and pray.

Having access to people and being in a position to hear them share any part of their lives with you, treat that time as church. We don't just gather at the assembly; we gather with those who need to see Christ and the Word working every day. So when you are at school, take the

Day 8

Word with you.

When you sing, dance, or write, use the superpower of the Word to supercharge the work of your hands. Don't feel like what you have has to hit the big screen for you to be on the radar of God. He sees you in the light and in the dark. How you treat people matters. How you look and sound–even how you serve others, He cares about.

Do you allow other people to interrupt your day–if the Father drops them into your lap and says pray for them? I cannot tell you how many times the Father has dropped a Word in my heart, and I will ask, "Excuse me, do you mind if I pray for you?" Just being available is enough for the Father to use you and make you His light that He puts on a lamp stand so that many can hear you and see you personify the goodness of God. It is not always the beauty you see in the person; it can also be the Good Lord's glory.

Have you been able to join the experience yet? Get my free emails and text messages to help you journey through this experience!

Question

Do you know that what you have is enough to impact nations? Something simple you do with your hands can bless others. What do you think that is for you?

Prayer

> "Holy Father, we thank You for sharing Your powerful Word with us. We thank You that Your breathing and living Word is saving and keeping us as we use our hands. We thank You for blessing us and reminding us to seek You in all that we do. If You invite us to share something with someone, we thank You for allowing Your Word and presence to be felt. We thank You for empowering us to speak to nations and be a light that You choose to shine on a lampstand. Prepare my heart, lifestyle, and mind to move in this promotion. Keep me mindful of You always as You elevate me on the job, in my business, career, and with relationships. In Yashua's name, hallelujah, and so be it."

Affirmation "Father, You are the light of the World, and I thank You for using me as a vessel of Your light for those I will impact."

Reflection

> *Where do you see the light of God shining? How can you use His superpower to impact how you use your hands?*

Notes

15 And let the peace of Christ rule in your hearts, to which indeed you were called in one body. And be thankful. **16** Let the word of Christ dwell in you richly, teaching and admonishing one another in all wisdom, singing psalms and hymns and spiritual songs, with thankfulness in your hearts to God. **17** And whatever you do, in word or deed, do everything in the name of the Lord Jesus, giving thanks to God the Father through him.

Day 9 Colossians 3:15-17

Day 9

It is not enough to be hearers and not doers of the Word. We are not cult followers who look to a person to give us all of our food and drink; we are independent thinkers, each gifted with a function in the body of Christ. We are to allow the peace of Christ to be with us and help us settle into the gift He has given us.

Before the foundation of the world, you were already thought of, and the Word was used to speak you into existence. Your purpose, gifts, and talents were already determined like any angel. But you were special in that, you were destined for earth, to come in the likeness of God. To have a mind, will, word–your spirit…soul has a mission.

We are not all the same, but we are to be of one faith, one mind, one baptism believing that there is only One God and Father of all, who is above all, through all, and in all who believe (Ephesian 4:5-6). The glue that joins believers in Him, and we can hear each other and take advice because He uses us to sharpen each of us (Proverbs 27:17).

The Father said He would never leave us ignorant of the enemy's devices (2 Corinthians 2:11). He will give us what we need to make educated, informed decisions, but are we listening? Are we allowing the Word of God and the people of God to usher us in the right direction? We are to encourage each other, think on things that are lovely, to sing, and preach sound wisdom. Do you feel that you're doing well with this assignment?

Day 9

This role is not just for the pastors. It is for the believer also. All who have the Spirit of Yah should be vessels for His use to use as His mouthpiece. You are more than a woman, a man, a person of color, or a person who speaks a language; you are a child of the Most High God, and He has plans for you!

His plan is to have you be His hand, heart, head, mouth, feet, and other elements of the body of Christ here on earth. To point to the Kingdom is what we should do and why we want Him to bless our work. We want to do all of our work to please the Father, to line up with the Word, so that we may be found blameless (2 Peter 3:4).

We cannot do this without the Spirit of Yah, the Word, living and breathing on the inside of us. We must have a lifestyle that gives the Father room to use us and help nations through us. We give thanks to the Father for the Word because the Word is the power by which anyone's life can be saved. The healing power of God is activated through His Word! The power we all need to perform our great work and to release the healing the world needs in the mind, spirit, and soul is all in Yashua (Jesus), the Word of Yah.

Don't be shy and don't be stingy. Speak the Word of life and give glory and thanks to God for His presence; glorify Him living among men.

Question

> *Can the Father use someone to speak to you? Do you honestly listen and receive from people? Do you feel that the Father is trying to tell you something right now? What? Who are His vessels in your life?*

Prayer

"We enter into Your gates with thanksgiving and Your courts with praise. We sing songs of Your goodness, power, and majesty. We thank You for the Living Word by which we have become sons and daughters of Yours. We celebrate the great work You have done through the Word and for all who choose to believe. Thank You, Father, for freeing us from our dreadful, hunting, and low selves. We give You all the honor we have to give to Your name. We say thank You for being mindful of us and allowing Your Word to dwell among men to heal and deliver. May we please You in the works of our hands today. In Yashua's name, peace and blessings."

Affirmation   *"I am being used for healing and releasing the great power of God on the earth through His Word, which saves, delivers, and sets free!"*

Reflection

> *What are you grateful for? What scriptures or Word have you used lately to impact peoples' lives? How have the lives around you been changing?*

Notes

11 But let all who take refuge in you rejoice; let them ever sing for joy, and spread our protection over them, that those who love your name may exult in you. **12** For you bless the righteous, O Lord; you cover him with favor as with a shield.

Day 10 Psalm 5:11-12

Day 10

The enemy tries to steal God's praise, doesn't he? He makes us feel like we are too old, dumb, or out of it to make an impact on our purpose. He tells us because we haven't been seen yet, we will never be seen. He makes us doubt who we are and who we are called to be. I want to encourage you that no matter how old you are, how long you have been working, or what you do, the Father is not done with you yet!

The favor on your life is still there. Just hold on and let Him work. You are not forgotten–He said He will repay anyone who sacrifices a thing for Him in this life and the one to come (Mark 10:30).

Your name is not at the bottom of the list because all the while, His favor has been working for you. Any of us can have a premature death. Any of us can get unexpected news. We could be homeless, jobless, careless, heartless, and the list goes on.

What is so good about Yah, even if these things happen, He still can make a way out of no way. He will bring you peace no matter if that is in a barn, shelter, car, or some other place. His plans are not ours, but His ways are higher, and achieve what He sent it out to do. He is not slack nor absent-minded about you. He sent His son for you and helped restore your connection with Him so we will never feel alone–ever!

This God right here, is able to do exceedingly

Day 10

and abundantly more than anything we can ask or think (Ephesians 3:20). Renew your confidence today; favor can rearrange your life in a moment, and it can sustain you through circumstances. When you should be sinking, you will swim. When you should be dead, you will live. When you should look like past failure, you will look and feel like a winner.

Favor defies natural order and brings in the supernatural. If you need a miracle, you need favor. When you realize the power of favor, you also have to acknowledge the power of praise and exultation.

You need to be in expectation for a miracle! The Father wants you to believe for it and work toward your belief! James said I will show you my belief based on my works (James 2:18). What are you believing for? What have you been working for?

I have to tell you, no matter what it looks like or how you may feel, exalt the name of the Lord. There is a blessing and a release–and here a Word concerning those who exalt the name of the Lord. By faith, we please God, and that is doing a work before you have the evidence. This is trust. We must trust God and operate in that when we exalt Him through any storm (Hebrews 11:1).

Those who sing to the Father have a special place in His heart. I sing to Him, and the way I hit notes doesn't matter. This is not a performance but an act of worship to release your gratitude to the Father in a way that He likes. Don't rob Him of your song, and withhold His favor. Walk in the blessing of His presence.

We all need the favor of the Lord because it affords us things we cannot always obtain. It speeds up a process, and it makes room for miracles. Be encouraged today if you need a miracle to help solve a problem. Your favor is here, sing a new song today.

Question

> *Where do you need the favor of God to show up? Do you believe favor is on your life? Can you recall a time when favor has been evident in your life?*

Prayer

> *"Father, give us favor to leap forward in our businesses, on our jobs, and in our careers. Thank you, Father, for giving back what the palmerworm, cankerworm, and caterpillar stole, as well as any other delay. Thank You for canceling the delay and monitoring spirits sent to spy out the plans and progress for our lives. Thank You, Father, for interrupting the plans of the enemy. Thank You, Father, that sickness, disease, mortality, and other spirits who You know their names sent to derail Your plans for my life are canceled. Thank You for being my shield and protecting me from the devourer, who roams around like a starved lion for the sheep of God. Thank You, Father, that the thief can steal no more! In Yashua's name, hallelujah, and so be it."*

Affirmation "The Father is redeeming my time, and anything I thought I lost, He has already restored."

Reflection

> The enemy thinks to steal, but he cannot stop the plans the Father has. Don't allow delays to stop your breakthrough or still your confidence. The Father got this! Just celebrate Him today and sing Him a song. Let me know what you sing.
>
> #drk21day

Notes

11 Whoever works his land will have plenty of bread, but he who follows worthless pursuits lacks sense. **12** Whoever is wicked covets the spoil of evildoers, but the root of the righteous bears fruit. **13** An evil man is ensnared by the transgression of his lips, but the righteous escapes from trouble.

Day 11 Proverbs 12:11-13

Day 11

What do you have in your hands, in your skill set that you can work to earn wealth and provide for yourself and your family? Have you noticed your talent poking through as you continue to advance in your career? Do you know there are talents born within you that you are commissioned to cultivate and will need you to be consistent in their development?

As we start working within our careers, it is important for us to determine what our gifts are. What talents do we have that will help us make life easier for ourselves? What do you enjoy doing? What is the work you perform that you want Yah to bless? Do you know that your hard work will turn a harvest in time? Verse 11 shows us that whoever works his land (gifts) will have plenty of bread. If you are willing to work, you are going to earn in heaven and on earth.

The question becomes, can you enjoy what you make? The curse many know too well is working hard and not being able to enjoy it. If you are working and not seeing the fruit, take the lessons you are learning and apply them. Everything you have and are learning will work to your good (Romans 8:28). Don't change that mindset, but keep it at the forefront of your mind. You have something this generation is waiting for, as Myles Monroe has said.

The key is you need to focus on where you are, yes, and not get caught up in get-rich-quick schemes. Anything telling you you don't have to work to earn money, raise an eyebrow, and investigate that more. We are called to work, it is a principle of God. It teaches lessons that only can be learned through appreciating what it takes to have something. If you feel that things come easy or free, you can misappropriate the value of a thing.

If we don't know how hard we need to work to obtain the wife or husband we have been praying for, we can abuse that spouse. If we don't know what it is like to have a child born that we desire, we can abuse or neglect that child. Understanding the value of a diamond will train us to protect it. We learn value through hard work. Chasing fantasies instead of working, the Bible says, is foolish and unwise. It is also unfruitful.

I can share with you a quick story about someone I worked with. He was a young man gifted with speaking with people and providing service. He was great at his job and was a top earner in sales. But he wanted more. He had ideas but lacked discipline. He felt that, based on his sales, he deserved a leadership role. But when he got the responsibility, he left early and didn't finish the job well.

He soon quit thinking he was too good for the job. He didn't see the value in hard work but thought they were wrong. He kept that same thought pattern everywhere he went while I worked with him. I told him the pattern he sees in his employment is a reflection of his work ethic. He thought he should advance based on sales alone. He didn't see the need to learn a business, and practice current steps, he wanted to come in and change everything to his liking.

In short, this mindset pushed him out of each business one after the other. This fast track he envisioned not only didn't exist, but it also robbed him of obtaining anything of lasting value. He made paychecks, but he didn't build a career. He had a slew of quits and firings behind him. Eventually, the choices caught up to him, and he asked the question, we all tried to get him to see. "Why do I think I can speed past process and progress?" It took him time, but he eventually got it. He had to work and build, brick by brick. Success is glamorous, but it is a process.

If you feel stagnant in your life, consider how you work. If you want the Father to bless your hands, you have to give Him something to work with, as my friend Melvina Washington says. It is wicked to covet the things of evildoers. Don't worry about what people are making on social media, tv, celebrities, or these fantasies we compare ourselves to. Focus on your level, your life, and let righteousness bear fruit.

Those who are lying, cheating, and doing ungodly things to earn wealth will be ensnared by the transgression of their own lips. They will get caught up in the mess they are in, but we are to escape these traps by keeping on the right road and doing right by people. The Father will reward you if no one else does.

Question

What are you building brick by brick? Do you have a strong foundation? Are you building up or simply moving around? Do you feel that your life is progressive?

Prayer

> "Father, You woke me up today, thank You. I am grateful for Your presence and confirmation that You will honor the works of my hand and all that I do to please You. Thank You for giving me favor with everyone—those who like me and those who don't. Thank You for stopping me from comparing myself to other people. Order my steps today to work and build on a strong foundation. Continue to help me make wise decisions that lead to building my house and not tearing it down. In Yashua's name, so be it."

Affirmation

> "I am building up my life one brick at a time and focusing on the step ahead—not as concerned with the end, but how I live my life to reach my end."

Reflection

> *Ask yourself: Am I working or being busy today? Am I building up my life or simply scattering my progress with how I live it? So far, what have you learned about yourself in this journey so far?*

Notes

5 And have you forgotten the exhortation that addresses you as sons? "My son, do not regard lightly the discipline of the Lord, nor be weary when reproved by him. **6** For the Lord disciplines the one he loves, and chastises every son whom he receives." **7** It is for discipline that you have to endure. God is treating you as sons.

Day 12 Hebrews 12:5-7

Day 12

Do you feel like you are being disciplined by the choices you have made in life? I remember my mom once pointed out a scripture that says if you are buffed (corrected) for your own fault, take it patiently (1 Peter 2:20). If you are currently in a learning or growth curve, don't get down on yourself. I know it can be very hard to deal with the consequences of our actions. Sometimes, we wish we could just hit control z or get a redo and not have to pay for the choices we have made.

I want to tell you that as a believer and child of Yah, you cannot escape all trouble and correction. Those whom the Father loves, He still corrects (Proverbs 3:12). If we go off the path, like any good parent, His job is to correct our steps. Sometimes, that means sitting us down to refocus our efforts. It could mean losing something we like or enjoy. Our choices do have consequences, so be mindful about how you live.

As children of Yah, we are to be the light to the world. We are good at enjoying being special and having privileges, but it can be challenging to embrace the responsibility. Along with the wealth of resources comes responsibility and accountability. It is not easy to have a harvest, is it? As a farmer quickly learns, you can plant a field of seeds, but if you are not diligent to care for the seeds they will not produce nothing for harvest season.

You will need to water the seed, pull the weeds, and keep bugs away if you want your plant to grow healthy and

Day 12

strong. When we take shortcuts, like spraying a pesticide, we can damage the very essence of what is inside. To fix one problem shouldn't create more issues. I once had a client who I was helping launch her bakery. She got a wonderful deal on a space, she was attached to a hair salon that stayed busy, and she started with curious customers.

We got everything going because she had recently gotten a settlement of about $25k that helped her front the expenses and her salary for about six months. This cushion made opening the business an easy choice, and she could relax as she built up the business. But before we got through month one, one of her daughters got into a financial pinch. She turned to her mother and asked for a $17k loan. She said she would pay it back and had an intention to do so.

How many of you know that life happened? She loaned the money to her daughter, the expenses for the business kept rolling in, and the money she loaned out removed her security blanket. She also had to run around to help others and had a few closed days a week. These choices to put other people's needs before her own led to clients having no trust in her business. She wasn't reliable in their eyes to be there. Her food wasn't the problem, and she had a good seed. Yet she failed to water and cultivate what she was building.

Although her daughter worked on paying her back and would eventually pay it off, the payments trickled in. With the days she was missing from work, her sales plummeted. Plus, she didn't have time to go around the neighborhood to promote her business to potential clients. Her lack of balance on time and loaning her reserves meant she had to be in several places at one time. She had to choose between helping her family and launching her business.

In short, she chose to be there for her family, and her business closed. To this day, she has not been able to secure a place and is in the same situation as before. She is still struggling to strike a balance with her family. Her family is comfortable with calling her and expecting her to change her plans to come and watch their children or help them in a financial pinch. She wants to show her daughters how to cook like her and do the great things in her mind, but none of them have an interest in learning.

She is so desirous to get out what she has inside her, that she would train anyone who cared to listen! Can you imagine how her children might treat her if she had invested more into her purpose and built up the business, and they could see the value of what she has? Too often, people--especially family, do not see the value of what you have. To be resourceful with food and find ways to make things new is invaluable to a mother, a wife, or people who want to feed themselves. She is remarkable with what she can do with dietary restrictions, ingredients, and ideas.

I am helping her again to organize her thoughts and ideas so we can work as partners to get this business off the ground. She is doing her part, putting her dreams first for the moment so that she can build a legacy for the children she loves for when she is gone. Legacy is not built overnight--but through a series of choices you make today, tomorrow, and throughout the years to come.

Question

What gifts or talents do you have? Have you started your business yet? What are the obstacles you are facing when telling people "no"? Are you the go-to for fixing problems in your family?

Prayer

> "We come to Your throne boldly to say thank You. To call You awesome, wonderful, and Wise Counselor. Father, we need your help to guide us in creating healthy boundaries with children, family, co-workers, habits, and other things competing for the time we need to fulfill our purpose and build a legacy. We thank You, Father, for not allowing us to fail the most important assignment in our lives as individuals: mothers, wives, fathers, or husbands. We thank You for Your direction and endless love to keep us as we make mistakes and helping us redeem that time like only you can. In your precious Son's name, Yashua (Jesus), we say thank you and hallelujah!"

Affirmation — "I trust You to help me create boundaries that I will follow to love myself and others, but importantly, You the most—and should I fail, thank You for redeeming my time."

Reflection

> *Where do I need to establish boundaries to protect my legacy? How can I best serve my family and fulfill my purpose? Is there anything else you want to share? Do you have a praise report? Write that down, too, in the notes!*

Notes

15 Six days shall work be done, but the seventh day is a Sabbath of solemn rest, holy to the Lord. Whoever does any work on the Sabbath day shall be put to death. **16** Therefore, the people of Israel shall keep the Sabbath, observing the Sabbath throughout their generations, as a covenant forever. **17** It is a sign forever between me and the people of Israel that in six days the Lord made heaven and earth, and on the seventh day he rested and was refreshed.'"

Day 13 Exodus 31:15-17

Day 13

If Yahweh, God Almighty, took a break to be refreshed on the seventh day, you, too, need to have a day where you take a rest. We are not robots constantly in play. During slavery, times of bondage when you don't control your time, you cannot avoid working as dictated by someone else. However, the free man/woman should work to honor this commandment.

We are to rest and not just spend the day lying around; ideally, we should pursue God to refresh ourselves. People who don't take breaks think they are getting ahead. The truth is your work becomes blah when you do things tired, burned out, or out of it. Taking breaks allows us to think clearer and work faster because our energy is restored; plus, we can see other perspectives.

Taking time to step back from a problem can help you solve it. I remember thinking I had to work the Sabbath to get ahead. I used to feel that any day was a work day. I allowed the enemy to convince me if I didn't work, I was being lazy. I felt guilty when I took a break, and the anxiety from not working would creep in and tell me I would be impoverished.

But how many of us know even though we work to make a living and fulfill our purpose, we must rest for the same reason? It would be best if you had a vacation, a break, or a day off to reflect on what you accomplished. When we take this time off, we give our brains time to reset. I started to take the Sabbath seriously in 2013. On my breaks, I would sit in the park for an hour and not feel any pressure during the day; I started to relax.

The anxiety I had about making money, I cut off and said to myself, "I cannot do anything about this right now. It is the Sabbath, and I will not work." I changed my work hours to state my policy and began to experience balance in my life. Having children, we think the most important thing is to afford them the necessities. I quickly learned it is about spending time with them and them knowing who you are and what you want to teach them as well.

Yes, working is important, but they remember more about your time with them. Most cannot tell you what they got last Christmas or three years back. Things don't hold a lasting impact like we think they would. But when you sit with them and help them with a problem, they remember that, and their soul will recall it when they need the advice again. This is a lasting impact.

I was missing out on things like that for my youngest in her very early years. I didn't want to repeat those mistakes for my other children as they grew older. I needed to change, take a break, and breathe!

We all need to step away from the cares of this life and meditate on things that are good, lovely, and bring peace. I realized the more I rested on the Sabbath, the more productive I became. There were times I felt I would miss a deadline because I couldn't work after sundown from Friday to Saturday at sundown. Do you know the Father would make a way where I did more work on one day than on previous days, and I not only reached my deadline but surpassed my expectations?

I used to have jobs that wanted me to work on days I wanted to participate in church functions. I was a server, and I said, "God, I can't go to church. They have me working every Sunday morning. If you want me to come, you are going to have to give me the day off."

Do you know I was off the next weekend! I didn't party all night Saturday to sleep in Sunday; I took myself to bed the same as normal and went to church that Sunday. I know the value of turning up to church and why I come is because the Father made a way for me to be there. I go to please Him and not man.

Question

Are you taking breaks to refresh your strength? You need your time, and you cannot apologize for taking the time to collect your thoughts. What will you do with your time? Try that today.

Prayer

> *"Thank You, God, for helping me today to learn the importance of rest. Help me to make time for You daily in my life and set aside a day a week to renew my strength. Thank You, Father, for easing and removing any anxiety I feel as I take these much-needed breaks. Thank You for taking my life in Your hands so I do not worry about what will be because my confidence is in You. Thank You for eliminating worry. Thank You for reminding me that I can trust You and rely on You for all my needs. Work will be there, and my relationship with You will build while I work and support my family and purpose. In Yashua's name, hallelujah!"*

Affirmation

"Today, I set aside time daily for You and also for myself one day a week, and during this time, I will remove all worries from my mind."

Reflection

> *What do you do for Yah and God alone? What arrangements or commitments have you made with Him that keep you faithful? Commit to taking out time for God daily, but also yourself, and break once a week for a day. Let me know what praise reports you have.*

Notes

9 Then he said to me, "The guilt of the house of Israel and Judah is exceedingly great. The land is full of blood, and the city full of injustice. For they say, 'The Lord has forsaken the land, and the Lord does not see.' **10** As for me, my eye will not spare, nor will I have pity; I will bring their deeds upon their heads."

Day 14 Ezekiel 9:9-10

Day 14

Have you ever felt like Yah didn't love you? That He doesn't see your struggle, and if He does, He could care less? Why do you think you feel this way? Is it because you didn't get what you wanted? Because you desperately needed to get out of a jam and were left in it?

God is above the earth, and He watches over us all. He is watching over not only our actions but also our thoughts, intentions, and motivations. He is all-knowing and all-seeing. He is above every situation and has a vantage many could never comprehend. None of us fully understand. He has to strike the perfect balance to allow man to choose and protect His chosen. He carries us when we make mistakes and keeps us from completely losing ourselves.

If it were not for grace, where would many of us be? No man is perfect, no not one (Romans 3:10-12). We all fall short of the glory of the Most High, but we should not give up on doing good because we fall short (Romans 3:23). We should not choose to stay in a life of sin or injustice because we feel we cannot win. Yah is watching how you react to wins, failures, challenges, and accessible opportunities.

Your attitude will determine your altitude! If you want to be great, you must learn how to have peace and calm in times of trouble. Paul said he had to learn to be content with being in want and having plenty (Philippians 4:12-13). We must not just hear the principle but apply it to our lifestyle. Your lifestyle is a choice. It is not who you are but who you work to become.

Like your wardrobe, you get to choose what you put on. You get to pick your clothes, shoes, and outfit. For those with a more particular taste, you can select your fabric, make your seam lines, sew them, and ultimately design your style. The style, nonetheless, is how you want others to perceive you and how you want people to see you. What is your lifestyle saying about you?

How we live our lives should reflect how we regard our beliefs. If we say we believe in the Father, we must reflect that belief in the good or bad times. If we say God is not here and He doesn't care, so I don't care. That is the wrong approach for His children.

We must humble ourselves and pull our emotions in to allow our spirit to conquer them. We have to say to our feelings, "peace be still." We have to choose a level heart and mind in times of trouble rather than acting out of our emotions. Because when Yah gets mad, His recourse is not one we can easily deal with. Keep Him calm, and submit yourself to His authority.

Question

> *Do you have a lifestyle that confirms your beliefs? Are you living a life of justice and righteousness, as if God was watching?*

Prayer

> *"Father, guide my emotions today. If I have ever felt angry towards You or taken an approach to say, You don't care about me, so I don't care about living right, please forgive me. Thank You for showing me today that You are worthy and more valuable than anything else for me. Please, Father, watch over me and help me to put my heart in the right place. Keep me in right step with You. In Yashua's name, so be it."*

Affirmation

"Father, You are in control of my life, and You have the authority to help my mind stay focused on You no matter the noise around me."

Reflection

> *What do you feel you need to hear today? How are you feeling? What can you share about your growth so far?*

Notes

13 "You are the salt of the earth, but if salt has lost its taste, how shall its saltiness be restored? It is no longer good for anything except to be thrown out and trampled under people's feet. **14** "You are the light of the world. A city set on a hill cannot be hidden. **15** Nor do people light a lamp and put it under a basket, but on a stand, and it gives light to all in the house. **16** In the same way, let your light shine before others, so that they may see your good works and give glory to your Father who is in heaven.

Day 15 Matthew 5:13-16

Day 15

Your gifts were given to you without repentance. You were born with gifts from the Good Lord above, and He wants you to use them to exemplify His character, goodness, and beauty on earth. Seeing people work in their gifts and knowing the value of their creations is wonderful. It is a joyful feeling to taste the works of someone's hands, and it leaves your mouth watering with flavor.

Have you ever tried a plate of food that was so good you couldn't help but rave about the taste? The textures were right, the warmth was right, and it was an experience you felt as you ate it. The food helps unlock an emotion you can barely put words to. You have unlocked a moment of happiness that you won't easily forget.

This is the salt that is born with you. This makes you unique, wonderful, and lovely. When you're aware of your gifts, talents, and purpose, you learn that you have a purpose to fulfill. Salt is used to flavor food, yes, but also as a preservative, a healing agent in the ocean, for cleaning, and much more. Salt has a taste and multiple functions. When salt is missing, what can you taste? How would your ancestors have preserved food? How would the fish live who need it in the waters?

So, what do you do with something that has lost its essence? Like containers that once held food or something in them, when they are empty, we toss them away, not seeing the value anymore in the container. The container has the same value, but when something prized and desired is

Day 15

inside, no one would think to throw it away.

You have what you need to do within you for what the Father has for you to do. You are valuable because you have something on the inside. If you are looking at a clear container, and inside that container, it is something that appears clear, you might think it is empty if you don't pick it up and handle it. How many of us see ourselves, and because what we see seems clear, we don't think anything is there. It is an illusion happening with our eyes.

If you have the light to be shared with the world to bring something into view, why would you hide under a basket? Why would you bury your gifts when you need them? Why would you stop talking when people need to hear what you have to say? Why would you stop writing when people need to read what you bring to the world? Why stop fighting for justice, to end hunger, or to lift people's spirits when people need you?

Keep your gift and talent alive, no matter what your gift is or how the Father has called you to show His goodness to the world. Please share it with the world by volunteering, working, or having a business that shares your talent. The Father wants to put you on a stand so people with eyes can see it and marvel at how good He is by making you. Embrace the light.

Question

> *What are you overlooking about yourself? How do you think you need to refocus your attention to notice those details?*

Prayer

"On today, we ask that You help us to see You clearly. That You keep us from missing Your power and gifts in our lives. We know that You have empowered us and given us special gifts that made it mandatory that we are put on earth! Thank You for calling me into existence and speaking my name into the Book of Life. Thank You for allowing me to live another day to spend time working my gift(s) and showing those around me Your love. You loved us so much that You sent me to them and them to me. We are all connected and need each other. Thank you for the Body of Christ that will work to share the Good News and how we all are the Salt of the Earth! In Yashua's name, hallelujah!"

Affirmation  "I will trust You to reveal my talents and help design a plan and situations that allow me to share my gifts with the world."

Reflection

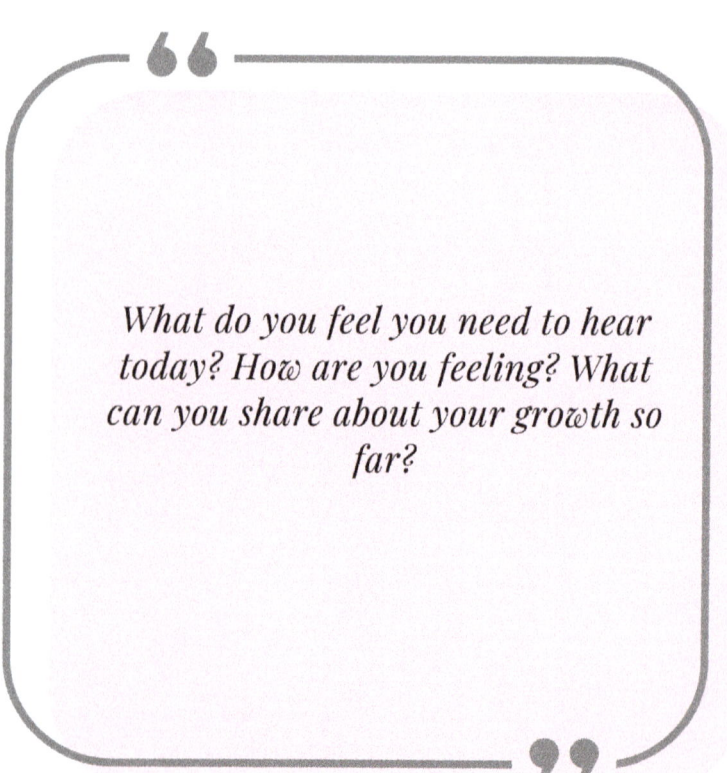

What do you feel you need to hear today? How are you feeling? What can you share about your growth so far?

Notes

29 Let no corrupting talk come out of your mouths, but only such as is good for building up, as fits the occasion, that it may give grace to those who hear. **30** And do not grieve the Holy Spirit of God, by whom you were sealed for the day of redemption. **31** Let all bitterness and wrath and anger and clamor and slander be put away from you, along with all malice

Day 16 Ephesians 4:29-31

Day 16

If you need the blessing on your life and for Father to bless the works of your hands, you need to be mindful of your words. Our words create life, the same as Yashua (Jesus) the Word in the flesh was used to create everything that is or will be. We have the power to use our words to create because we are made in the likeness of Yah.

You are a powerful being, far more powerful than your circumstances. You can overcome the spirit of confusion, manipulation, familiar spirits, monitoring spirits, and others who like to cluster together to circumvent the plans Yah has for us. Don't let them take your peace of mind. You were born for a time such as this!

For some of us, our hands are not the issue for why the blessing is not seen. Our mouth blocks the plans He has and delays our season of increase. Suppose you have been working hard on your job to get a promotion. Don't you let corruptive talk come from your mouth. Don't say, "They don't like me." "They don't see how hard I work." Or that "They don't care about what I am doing." These are negative statements that you spoke that can be used against you by the enemy.

He wants to use your words against you and make your worst dreams come true. He loves to feed on your fears and try his best to make them your reality. Sometimes, it is not the enemy creating the environment, but our words shaping how we will respond to the inevitable. If you are on a boat headed to the waterfall, you cannot say, "See, this

Day 16

is what I thought was going to happen." You were simply on the boat, and the focus should not be on thinking away the waterfall but on how you will deal with the situation and make the best of it.

Sometimes, we are in situations that are not our fault. We can do everything right, but we still miss the mark. But if I can tell you this, sometimes you need to call out what it is, so you can prepare for how to respond. When the Titanic was sinking, prayers to keep it afloat were not the priority. Surviving the sinking ship was the focus because it would sink no matter what. In our lives, people are going to die. No matter how good you are or how sincere you pray, we all will eventually die.

We don't pick the timing; the God over time does. We have to be careful not to speak words of murder, saying things like, "I wish they would just die," or anything similar. We are to keep talk like that from our lips. We are to speak words that build up people and help them stay strong during the times of tests. If you are on the job, giving it all you got, and you are not seen for your work, your work might need a bigger stand!

When you feel wronged, don't bad-mouth people and spew malicious words against them. Choose to remain blameless. It is okay to leave a company in search of better opportunities. It is okay to make your own job, if the jobs you work refuse to pay your value. It is okay to team up with others to ease the burdens and be open to working together.

Let go of bitterness you might hold from people or organizations that have wronged you. Choose to clear your heart and mind so that you will be whole. You don't want to grieve the Holy Spirit, no, by speaking reckless words.

You need to be mindful of how what you speak shapes your world. Don't curse God because things might appear slow. We don't always know how He will respond to our attacks against Him. It could be like the Tower of Babel, where He killed those on the top, or He shows mercy. The best action is to be out of the seat of judgment.

Share your feedback and journey so far! Join the conversation and use the online resources at

AuthorKLee.com/bless-works-of-my-hands-21-day

Question

What in your life has been overlooked? Are you in the right atmosphere to be seen? Are you in the right frame of mind and positive about what you have to offer?

Prayer

> *"Thank you for opening my eyes and heart to release all bitterness I carried toward jobs, co-workers, family members, children, and others who have done me wrong. Help me to forgive so that I may have peace and good health. Keep me from looking at life only from one perspective. Help me to see things like You do and be considerate of others. Show me when it is time to move. Bless me in the place in which You want me to remain, and show me where to go if not here to be in Your will for my life. Thank you for Your direction and protection through all things, in Yashua's name, so be it."*

Affirmation

> *"I am not the lord over time, and I don't get to pick and choose every event, but whatever is in my hands to do, I will do my best to respond with the right heart and love through the good and bad times."*

Reflection

> What do you feel you need to hear today? How are you feeling? What can you share about your growth so far?

Notes

32 And now I commend you to God and to the word of his grace, which is able to build you up and to give you the inheritance among all those who are sanctified. **33** I coveted no one's silver or gold or apparel. **34** You yourselves know that these hands ministered to my necessities and to those who were with me. **35** In all things I have shown you that by working hard in this way we must help the weak and remember the words of the Lord Jesus, how he himself said, 'It is more blessed to give than to receive.'

Day 17 Acts 20:32-35

Day 17

We cannot be hypocrites and tell others, specifically our children, to work hard, get an education, and do good, and great things will come your way if we don't do that, too! We don't want to profess that hard work will get you far, and then don't practice it ourselves. People watch what we do more than what we say. It is easy to say anything, but to do great work takes strength.

When we are willing to work out our soul salvation and allow Yah to complete a great work in us, we will get an inheritance reserved for those who are sanctified. We might think this inheritance means we will wear a Roli, drive a Benz, wear the latest fashions, or live in a big house. But the inheritance of God is not that. To Him, clothes are clothes, although He knows the price tag. A house is a house; it keeps you from being homeless. A car is a means of transportation. A watch tells time, and your phone can do that, too!

We have many ideas for why we need things or want them. The Bible says He will give us the desire of our hearts (Psalm 37:4). If we look at the verses surrounding this one, we will find that this is the Word for those who commit their way to the Lord (v3). Those who are faithful and commit their lives to justice will be revealed (v 6-8). There is more to context than what we read in an isolated verse.

What is the inheritance of God? An inheritance is a wealth transfer of what you get because of your lineage and

Day 17

a gift from a family member. Yashua (Jesus) said we are joint heirs with Christ (Romans 8:17). What He has done for us, He has done in our place. He is the propitiation, the payment, for our sins. He suffered the punishment we should have. He paid the bill we racked up. He came in and redeemed us.

Redemption means to pay in full and restore someone whole (Dictionary.com). Your sins have been paid for, bought with a high price, and you are restored whole to enter His eternal rest. Sinners do not have a place in heaven. Those who have sinned are forgiven because Yahwah's required payment was already paid. You are not only saved for heaven, you are sealed here on earth!

The blessing of Christ is that He is the living Word. The Word of God walked on earth and lived amongst men, women, and children. We could interact and even touch the face of the Word of God! How powerful to touch ages. To touch the vessel God Almighty created to be used to create everything that has ever been and will be. How wonderful is that!

The greatest example Yashua did for humanity was give. He gave His life as a ransom, but He also spent His time on earth giving to people (Mark 10:45). He gave the sermon at the mount. He healed the eyes of the blind, gave the mute speech, and helped the lame walk (Matthew 11:5)! He cleansed the leapers (Matthew 8:1-14). He forgave the sins of the woman caught in the act of adultery (John 8:1-11). He showed mercy and was encouraging. He brought back the dead and healed the sick (Matthew 10:8).

He gave and is still giving. He gave His Word to

still perform these acts and even left His Spirit so we didn't have to wait for the Glory to be put on us; it now dwells within us! If this doesn't make you tear up joyfully because of His goodness, you might not understand all He has done. Greater works are we able to do because of what He has done (John 14:12). Salvation is your inheritance, forgiveness, mercy, hope, joy, peace, love, kindness, and so much more (Isaiah 12:2, Romans 10:9, Ephesians 2:8-9, John 3:16, 1 Thessalonians 5:9).

Question

Are you committed to the way of the Lord? What do you think the inheritance of God is?

Prayer

> *"Father, You are good, and I thank You for sending Your Son to redeem me from my sins. Yashua, Jesus the Christ, You have delivered me from my sin. You have been the payment for my wrongs. You were bruised because of my choices. I thank You for making me aware of how I live and my choices and how they contributed to what You went through on the cross. I will not keep overlooking the payment You paid and treat it as a minor thing. I want to love You all of my days and never lose the inheritance that Yashua has afforded me and that You gave to all who believe. Thank you for salvation, forgiveness, mercy, hope, joy, peace, love, and Your kindness."*

Affirmation — *"I am saved by grace, loved by God, and filled with His joy, peace, kindness, hope, and mercy."*

Reflection

> *What has spoken to you today about this entry? How do you see Christ, the Messiah?*

Notes

22 Do not rob the poor, because he is poor, or crush the afflicted at the gate, **23** for the Lord will plead their cause and rob of life those who rob them. **24** Make no friendship with a man given to anger, nor go with a wrathful man, **25** lest you learn his ways and entangle yourself in a snare.

Day 18 Proverbs 22:22-25

Day 18

As believers, we are to have a heart for the poor and those who need help. We shouldn't be judgmental and seek to exploit their weaknesses. Too often, people are signing away their lives and never reading contracts. People will give us a summary of the document, and for the most part, they may be honest with that, but they don't tell you what could harm or impact you. We have blind faith when we trust people and take on agreements, thinking everyone would be fair.

We don't have to look far, however, to see that isn't true. Many people believe in the healthcare system and their oaths to be good to people. Then you hear of stories where doctors signed off on treatment plans for people who didn't need it. Greed can make people look at others as dollar signs, not humans. The poor will be with us always, was said in the bible (Matt 26:11). So there are many reasons why we end up in this condition, and it is a part of life.

Sometimes wars happen, and that robs you of the things you have. The stock market can tank, and your wealth can go out the door. You can have other things go wrong that can render you penniless, too. So, being fair to those without is a great lesson because you might be on the receiving end. So many doctors and wealthy people are beggars on the street now or they are sick and need help now. You can talk to them, and some don't ever want to go home or go back to the work they did before.

We may think we should feel sorry for them, but

Day 18

many would tell us not to. The Lord will fight the battles of those who call on Him, no matter where you find yourself, in your right mind or not, rich or poor, homeless or in a house. He can bring healing and restoration to us all. He can fight any battle and restore anyone to wholeness. This is what makes the Gospel good news!

If you are poor in spirit, the Father knows how to reach out and save you. The Father will judge those who exploit people after breakups, deaths, or trouble comes. He will convict you for harming people while they are down. It is wrong when people are not in their right mind, and folks have them sign their lives away.

For men and women eaters, the Father doesn't like that. If somebody has done you wrong, don't worry; the Father will avenge the poor. I have heard of people whose hearts were broken when their husbands died. This particular woman I am thinking about was a preacher's wife. When her husband died, within thirty days, the church kicked her out of the house they provided for her family to live in.

I understand you have to move the new family somewhere, but I think there should be a provision for the deceased pastor's family. This man gave his life to help others with their families, and now that his family is in need, to kick her out with no resources looks pretty wrong to me. I pray for the many who have had to experience this and that the Father restores the family and heals any hurt within their hearts.

The danger with hurt people and those with unresolved pain is that it can turn to unrighteous anger. Angry people can think of too many things to seek their own justice and steep into a wrathful path. People like this are dangerous, and they tend to bring others on this rampage. The Father tells us to stay away from people taking their pain out on others. These are people who can bully others and try to control other people.

A person with a vengeful heart can easily give into the spirit of control, lying, and manipulation. Try to avoid people acting out their frustration in negative ways like this. Hurt people can hurt other people.

If you have a problem with your brother, it is better to try to work it out with them (Matthew 18:15-17). If, after you have tried that, they are still hateful and malicious, leave it in God's hands to clear up and remove yourself. No one deserves to be dragged on a vengeful and hurtful journey to no avail. No one can give you what they do not have.

Question

Are you poor in spirit or finances today? Where do you need to lean on the riches of God for your life?

Prayer

> "If I have a plan to do anyone harm because I am hurt, forgive me, Father. If my poor spirit or finances are causing me to be bitter and speak negatively, Father cancel my words and make those words unfruitful. Thank you for not allowing words I said in anger to plague me for the rest of my life. Forgive me, Father, and teach me how to be more mindful of my words. Keep me from making mistakes that could cost me valuable relationships. Show me how to be more like you and have a heart of mercy and grace. Teach me to have a heart for the poor and want to work issues out with others. In Yashua's name, so be it."

Affirmation "Any wrongs people have done to me, I forgive, and I will keep a soft heart that allows me to create healthy boundaries to forgive and move on."

Reflection

> *Do you have unresolved issues of pain in your life? How have you dealt with pain in the past? Do you need God to heal your heart?*

Notes

18 There is no fear in love, but perfect love casts out fear. For fear has to do with punishment, and whoever fears has not been perfected in love. **19** We love because he first loved us. **20** If anyone says, "I love God," and hates his brother, he is a liar; for he who does not love his brother whom he has seen cannot love God whom he has not seen. **21** And this commandment we have from him: whoever loves God must also love his brother.

Day 19 1 John 4:18-21

Day 19

Love, we all need it. Eighty-year-olds are quick to say they need it. Babies cry for it and yearn to feel loved. My four-year-old asks me daily, "Mommy, do you love me?" Each time I say, "Yes, Mommy loves you." Sometimes, I think to spice up my answer and say, "Yes, Mommy loves you, and I will never stop loving you."

Now he sings, "Mommy loves. Mommy loves me. She will never stop loving me." It is the cutest thing when he does it, I do tell you. I am going to try to record it so you can believe me. He often pops up out of the blue when he asks the question.

Through my son, I found that we all need to hear, "I love you. You are loved. I will never stop loving you." These simple phrases need to be etched on our hearts so that when we want to run, feel fear, or see doubt, we can bate it down and say, "God loves me, and He will never stop loving me." We need to sing and dance when we say it, too!

The joy of the Lord is our strength (Nehemiah 8:10). When we find joy in God's love, we have found the root to anchor our lives. His love is like no other. He will love us and remove fear, help us with long suffering, patience, kindness, and care. Yah gives us something in exchange for our pain. He gives us His beauty for our ashes (Isaiah 61:3).

We learn to love by looking at how God loves us.

Day 19

He loves us unconditionally and is always reaching out to us to extend his goodness. He is mindful of us and makes provision for us. Love is not a reaction; it is a prompt that makes you act! Love will have you work, and it will not feel like work. It will help keep you from becoming resentful and hateful toward those you love.

Love keeps a right heart in us. Love chases away envy and strife, making you want to achieve peace. Love will push you to believe in the good and not rely on evil to make amends. Love will release you and bring your anxiety level to zero. If you are anxious, mad, or need to drop baggage, connect with the love of Yah. Many things will not matter as much as they did–not because you no longer care but because you have been healed!

The pain from a healed wound is no longer there, even if there is a mark to show that it used to be. Only open wounds and those that have not healed still bleed and cause the most discomfort. We can try to force healing, close a wound, or put something else in it besides the love of God, and the pain will resurface–the wound can open up again. We can heal wrong, and that causes more problems than we had at first.

Letting God into your heart, life, direction, family, business, career, and thoughts brings love to your problem. Love judges, but it also forgives. Love is honest; it doesn't lie but points to a solution. Love acknowledges where things are and where they can be. Love is progressive and wants to see you grow up and move on. Every situation can teach us something, but to many, we allow it to hold us back. Love sets you free!

To be like Christ, we must learn to love those we see. We learn to love those we see because that helps us to understand our condition. Any of us can fail, and all of us were in a life of sin before we were saved. When we can find a way to love our brothers and sisters, we do see ourselves. We learn to see things similarly to Yahweh.

It is not easy to love those who persecute you, no. Yet, learning it helps you become more like God. Judging sin and casting out demons, He does. Being a righteous judge, we also must become and casting out spirits as He teaches us.

We have to allow our hearts to grow like the Grinch so we can enlarge our territory. With a heart too small, we cannot include the people He sees as children of God. Like Jonah, many people in the Bible saw people's errors perfectly when they thought to judge them. But he, too, found out what mercy was.

In his judgment of Nineveh, a wicked nation, he learned that if the Father had no mercy, he too would have been killed. Rebellion is like the spirit of witchcraft (1 Samuel 15:23).

Question

Do you need a heavenly exchange? Are you carrying hurt, pain, or things that are weighing you down today? Get lighter, write them down and lets pray about it!

Prayer

"Gracious God, thank you for having mercy on me. I have needed your forgiveness so much. My heart is to remain open to Your lead. I will be open to forgive because people with unforgiveness in their hearts cannot make it into heaven. Please help with the heavy burdens on my heart today. And I commit to not live my life here on earth in the spirit of rebellion and forfeit the Kingdom of Heaven. I desire to be more like you. Help me in areas where I struggle to forgive. Help make my heart soft. Show me love and allow me to accept it from where You send it. Teach me to reject lust that pretends to be love. Teach me to know what flattery is and to reject it also. Thank You Father for Your guidance, in Yashuah's name, so be it."

Affirmation   *"I trust Yah to heal my heart and keep me from rebellion against His plans for my life and family."*

Reflection

> *Are you operating in rebellion? Is there someone you need to forgive? Have you done all you can to right relationships? Have you put them into the hands of God and freed yourself from the guilt? Release the pain and allow Him to heal.*

Notes

4 But I am the Lord your God from the land of Egypt; you know no God but me, and besides me there is no savior. **5** It was I who knew you in the wilderness, in the land of drought; **6** but when they had grazed, they became full, they were filled, and their heart was lifted up; therefore they forgot me.

Day 20 Hosea 13:4-6

Day 20

Sometimes, we say dangerous words like, "I don't know how I made it, but I am here." What do you mean you don't know how you made it? Is it that we don't know how we made it, or we don't want to acknowledge who helped us? We all know when we haven't done things on our own, and truthfully, we never do anything alone. We need power!

God said he would give us the power to get wealth (Deuteronomy 8:18). Nothing we have, we got alone. We all needed favor from Yah to acquire what we have. Even the kingdom of darkness cannot trespass where the Father draws a line. Nature cannot reroute His design. The Atlantic and the Pacific will never blend because He set it in motion. He will not share His glory with another–ever.

He is the reason we breathe. Do you know when man became a living soul, it was because He breathed life into his body? One breath was enough to fuel the breath of all humanity. He doesn't have to breathe into each of us when we breathe in and out. He doesn't have to give us breath at birth--it is already there! He did this thing once, and it keeps on giving.

The Garden of Eden is like that. It keeps on giving, and there is no end. We want the fountain of youth because our bodies know we shouldn't age, but we must because He limited the gift He gave. In our new bodies, we will not age. We will achieve what man is willing to kill for: an endless supply of life.

Day 20

Life belongs to the Father, and no one else can give it. He provides the soul, and He creates your gifts and talents. He is the great architect, and *nothing* is without His design. When falling angels thought to create without His permission, He killed their bodies. When man decides to invent and produce hybrids, if his creation does not please Yah, He will kill it in His timing (like broccoli, haha!).

He is above the earth and all vessels, small and large. We cannot do anything without His knowledge. Many plans are eliminated before seeing the light of day because He blocks access. Angels are bound still in hell because He said they would remain. He is all-powerful, and *nothing* is too hard or beyond His reach!

When man needs help, even the nonreligious calls on God. We can talk and say we don't know Yah and that there is no God, but when fear grips you. When the ultimate doom seems to be inevitable, and we see death, we know that death is real. When we see hell, we know it is real. When we see demons and witches act out, we know or pray that there is a God!

We seek Yah during times of drought. When the earth is hell on earth, we pray that there is a heaven somewhere. We pray to God, who can deliver. We call on the One who saved us before when we didn't know what to do. We ask Him to do it again, and again, and again. The danger is that we can soon forget who got us here if we are not careful. We can look at what we have and forget the One that got us here.

So what happens when God blesses the works of your hands? Will you keep serving Him? Will you stay not

171

working the Sabbath? Will you continue to put Him first, being a good spouse or loving parent? Will you keep making time for the things and people who matter most?

Or will you be like the many who get full, attain wealth, make money, and forget all about God and family? Will you buy clothes, shoes, and vacations instead of retirement plans? Will you buy things that will spoil instead of investing? Will you eat the seed Yah has given you instead of planting it so your children and grandchildren will have something?

Will you live your best life now and forget about the future? We must never forget that the same God that saved us from destruction and financial ruin is the same One that wants a tithe! If he asked for it all, would you give it to Him? Do you know what God did to Abraham? He gave Abraham immeasurable wealth and then asked for it all back! Yah asked for him to kill Isaac, his son, his legacy, the one who would get everything from him when he died. He asked for everything back from him!

And you know the response? He didn't hesitate to return it; the Lord saw his heart and gave him more! He gave Abraham what he already had and multiplied it. God gave Abraham more sons than the grains of sand. Abraham didn't abandon Yahweh because he had it all. He knew who his Source was, and he didn't want to cut off life even if he cut out his son. Are you willing to do that for God? Will you give what He asks of you or try to negotiate?

Obedience is greater than sacrifice (1 Samuel 15:22).

Question

Do you see Yah as King? How do you see Him (God) compared to your problems? Do you think they are something the Father has no plan to overcome? Who's in control?

Prayer

"God Almighty, You are my source. I am grateful that whatever I need today, you have supplied. I thank you for my house, money, family, and the means to supply answers to problems I face. Thank you for keeping me during my season of drought. Thank you for getting me this far. Thank you for keeping me in the right mind toward you. Thank you for putting good people in my life that will encourage me to do the same. Father, you are my best friend, my father, my protector, and my source for anything I need, and you define who I am. With gratitude in my heart, I pray and tell You, thank You. Hallelujah, and so be it."

Affirmation   *"I will lack no good thing because my Father in Heaven supplies it to me, and because of His faithfulness, I will remain true to my word and serve Him all the days of my life."*

Reflection

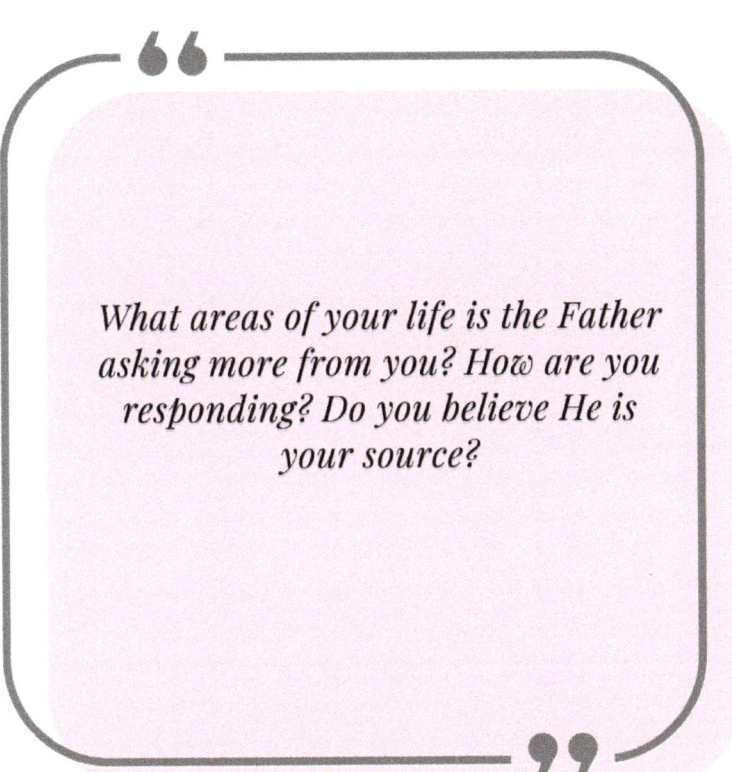

What areas of your life is the Father asking more from you? How are you responding? Do you believe He is your source?

Notes

1 Return, O Israel, to the Lord your God, for you have stumbled because of your iniquity. **2** Take with you words and return to the Lord; say to him, "Take away all iniquity; accept what is good, and we will pay with bulls the vows of our lips. **3** Assyria shall not save us; we will not ride on horses; and we will say no more, 'Our God,' to the work of our hands. In you the orphan finds mercy." **4** I will heal their apostasy; I will love them freely, for my anger has turned from them. **5** I will be like the dew to Israel; he shall blossom like the lily; he shall take root like the trees of Lebanon; **6** his shoots shall spread out; his beauty shall be like the olive, and his fragrance like Lebanon. **7** They shall return and dwell beneath my shadow; they shall flourish like the grain; they shall blossom like the vine; their fame shall be like the wine of Lebanon.

Day 21 Hosea 14:1-7

Day 21

Sometimes, we need a reminder of what is important, don't we? We must know that our jobs, marriages, businesses, stock markets, and other things are also not our Source! Our Source is the God of all things, above all the earth, who has all things in His hands. He is the God of life, and He knows the plans He has for us.

In life, there are always people sent to use their influence to prevent us from living the exemplary life. We may think I cannot make it if I don't have this. I am done for if I don't have money, a mother, father, job, career, or business.

Thank you, Father, for reminding us what is essential in life–You! It is because of you we can move when we are bound. That our minds can dream even when we don't see or know how something will happen. You take the limits off of life.

Today, we need to be reminded that our future is not limited by what we have seen, are used to, or what has happened before. You can rewrite our history and change our future. You can direct our path and make every crooked path straight (Luke 3:4-6). Father, You are good; because of You, we can believe in the greater.

We can ask You to bless the works of our hands because we know You care about us! We can ask You for wisdom if we don't see a thing because Your Spirit will reveal everything. You will not leave us ignorant of the enemies'

Day 21

devices. Thank you for being mindful of me and showing me Your goodness. It is when I return to Your Word that I am the most found, that I have hope and a future!

Thank you, Father, for saving me from myself. Thank you for helping me see your goodness when everything around me was not projecting it. Thank You for the light that has healed my heart and renewed my mind. Thank You for saving me and helping me to know that I am not an orphan. Even though people might have let me down, abandoned me, or left me to fend for myself, You are here with me.

I must lift up a praise to reach Your nostrils that demonstrate my gratitude for You fighting battles for me to get me this far. Thank You for not leaving me when I left You. Thank you for separating my sins as far as the East is from the West!

Thank you for allowing me to start over with You and creating my life anew! Thank You for not keeping me somewhere I deserved to be because Your mercy delivered me from the enemy's plans. Thank You for clearing up the fog in my heart and mind.

When we give our lives to Christ, we start to see His goodness. When we stop leaning on our own works, ideas, and plans and trust His, we can let go of the oppressors. We can leave jobs that do nothing for our souls. We can turn down marriage proposals that mean us no good. We can deny those who want us to steal, kill, or do things to harm others. We can choose a righteous path. We can live with conviction and purpose.

When we dwell under the wings of the Almighty, we can fly with You and be sheltered as we go to higher heights. As You take our lives and elevate us, we won't fear the altitude. We won't look at our appearance or second guess our gifting.

We won't get puffed up but humble ourselves to seek Your will first. Like a mature tree, we will be planted in Your word and love. We will know Your love and share that with others.

The fame that comes from our gifts, business, talent, ideas, and works of our hands, we will give You the glory You deserve. We will acknowledge You before man. We will put no other god before You! We will continue to adore You and sing, read, and pray.

Holy, holy, holy is our Lord God Almighty (Revelation 4:8)! You are mighty in battle, strong, and there is nothing You can't or won't do for me (Psalm 24:8). You love me, and I love You. I will continue to live as a testament to how good You are to those who love You.

Have you given this devotional a review yet? Or shared parts of your story with me? If not, please do. I would love to hear from you!

AuthorKLee.com/review

Question

How are you feeling today? Are you light as a feather or heavy as a rock sinking to the bottom of the ocean? Let us get aligned with what God is doing!

Prayer

> "As we finish this devotional, let this not be the end but the beginning of our committed-covenant life with you. Help us to go from here to where you see for us to grow to next. Don't let our efforts be in vain. Help this moment and all these days to impact my life in days to come. Help me to keep my mind on the principles and commandments I have learned to shape my lifestyle. Give me the heart, mind, and will to live a covenant life with you, Father. Thank you for your promises and power to uplift my spirit and works to reach high esteem. Help me never to forget You and to acknowledge You in all of my ways. In Yashuah's name, we pray, hallelujah, and so be it."

Affirmation   "I will live a covenant lifestyle where I put Your Word above my thoughts and others who will tell me otherwise."

Reflection

> *Today, I want you to be personal with Yah (God). I want you to reflect on everything we have done over the past few days and commit to continuing this journey. You can move on to the 30-day devotional or my book of prayers that will help you move to the next level in your journey. I encourage you to develop a prayer and study life to continue this great work. But jot down highlights from this journey, praise reports, and other things that come to mind as we wrap up day 21 or your last day in this devotional in your notes!*

Notes

> *Dr. Krystal Lee*
> *"Dr. K"*
>
> *@AuthorKLee*

"God blesses those who work for peace, for they will be called the children of God." Matthew 5:9

Dr. Lee has authored over thirty books across more than seven genres: adult, children, youth fiction, self-help, spiritual growth, novels, business, empowerment, etc. to help people in their most profound times of need.

She is also passionate about coaching programs and web courses she created for WAE (Write Anything Easily) Process, Embrace Your Crown, Turn Key Solution for Small and New Businesses, Transform Go Beyond Change (Personal Development, and The Lesson for youth and teenagers

Connect with me at

AuthorKLee.com

AuthorKLee.com
Creator of *WAE Process*

 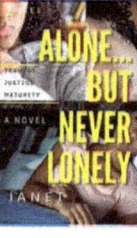    

    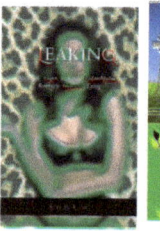 

KLEPub.com Authors

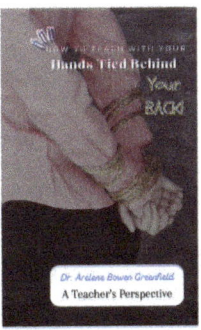

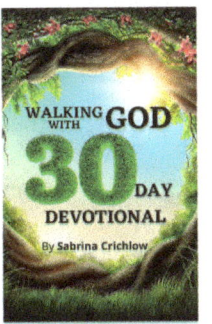

SCAN ME

It's time to start and finish **YOUR Story!**

KLE Publishing specializes in helping people become authors. In as little as 15 to 90 days, we can help you develop your book and publish to 39,000 outlets!

Ghostwrite, Edit, Format, Publish
We can help from **Start to Finish.**

Scan and fill out the short form to learn more and connect with us.

www.ingramcontent.com/pod-product-compliance
Lightning Source LLC
Chambersburg PA
CBHW061758070526
44586CB00023B/2625